POETRY IS THERAPY

Life beyond the Dark Clouds

Bruce Jacob Blada

jdt
Publications

First Edition: June, 2018

The moral right of the author has been asserted.

Published by JDT Publications
Port Moresby, National Capital District, Papua New Guinea
Email: jdtpublications@gmail.com

National Library of Papua New Guinea
Cataloguing-in-Publication entry:

Blada, Bruce Jacob. 1985 — .
    Poetry is Therapy: Life beyond the Dark Clouds.
    p. ; cm.

    ISBN-13: 978-9980-901-76-7

1. Poetry, Papua New Guinea.
i. JDT Publications.   ii. Title.
PNG/821/B52 – dc22

Printed in USA by CreateSpace Independent Publishing.

To my mother…thank you for everything.
To my little boy BJ…for bringing me so much happiness.

Thank you Michael Tawarot Kurumop for your assistance in editing and proof-reading the original draft. Also, thank you for giving me permission to include your poem 'Addiction' in my collection.

Special thanks to Jordan Dean for his assistance in publishing this book. His persuasion for me to publish my collection of poems and encouragement is greatly appreciated.

CONTENTS

FOREWORD

Prose and poetry are two sides of the same coin. Both of them communicate ideas, and both of them can be written beautifully. But the essential purpose of prose is to communicate ideas, and the essential purpose of poetry is to move us with the beauty of its crafted language, and in this distinction the two diverge. Prose is communication; poetry is art.

'Poetry is Therapy' is a reflection of the author's life, a person in search of the meaning and purpose of his existence. There is some truth in the poetic prose that will move the reader.

This collection portrays the author's quest to use poetry as an 'oasis in the desert' of pain, struggles and hopelessness.

Everyone has their own of way dealing with and overcoming challenges in life. This collection provides a voice of assurance that there's hope and a better life beyond the dark clouds.

The reader can identify and connect with the author through his eloquent writing shedding light upon topics that are most too often left reserved. A journey of self-discovery awaits as you begin to open the pages of this prose.

The author tries to keep an open intuition towards philosophical values, apparent by his crude perception of life; expressing views that are not only literal, but also connotations of foundational themes such as equality, love, and hope. The prose entails life as not only been pessimistic, but rather utopian, one that betroths hope.

Michael T. Kurumop

BEYOND THE DARK CLOUDS

Misery comes raining down
A torrential down pour of pain and misery
Falls on me and soaks me through
I shiver and take cover
I can't see the sun
Oh, how I crave its warmth.

But rain can't go on forever
Nor does winter lasts forever
All will cease and fade in time
Cause time give all things their moments
And the sun will come out and shine again
In all its glory and splendor.

Even though the clouds are dark
Even though the rain is falling
The sun is still shining
Beyond the dark clouds.

Man has never tried to look
Beyond the dark clouds
And see the sun shinning
Man has never nurtured the hope
That there are better days
And a better life
Beyond the dark clouds.

But the plants and trees know better
They stand tall, always reaching up
They know the sun is still shining
Beyond the dark clouds.

Depression

The grass ain't green no more
Like it used to be
The sky ain't blue no more
Like it used to be.

The sun is always hiding
Behind the dark grey clouds
From morning 'till evening
I know it's there but I never see it.

The world has lost its color
All I see is black and white
Nothing makes sense anymore
Nothing interests me anymore.

Therefore, I ask myself these two questions:
Did the world change?
Or just my perception of it?

WHO CAN SAVE ME?

Sad without reasons
Lonely amidst companion
I am depressed.

Painfully shy, always self-conscious
Socially anxious, low self esteem
I am a shy guy.

Panic thoughts, always anxious
Rapid heartbeat, sweaty and unsteady
I am a coward.

Second guessing, always uncertain
Faithless, always expecting the worse
I am a doubter.

Easily hurt, very sensitive
Prone to anger, violently unstable
I am a loose cannon.

The shackles of pain bind me
The chains of misery imprison me
I drown in the sea of oppression
I sink with the weight of depression
To the lowest depths of turmoil
I enter the gates of hell
And read the plaque Dante saw:
'Abandon all hope he who enters'.

Has my fate already been decided?
Is this cursed life my lot?
Is there hope for my salvation?
Who can save me?

STRANGER IN THE REAL WORLD

Childhood days, teenage years
Strict parents, over controlling
Christian parents, overprotecting
Religious dictatorship.

Rap music?
Censored and banned
Heavy Metal?
'Devil's music!'
PG movies?
'Shut that TV off!'

'Go to church! Read the Bible!'
'Do you want to go to hell?'
'Do you want to miss the Rapture?'

Consequences of disobedience?
Grounded, no TV, no dinner.

No swearing, no talking back
No smoking, no drinking alcohol
No dating, no mating
No memories of good old days.

Years later, early twenties
Liberation, Independence
Freedom at last
Yet still traumatized
Low self-esteem, doesn't fit in
Insecure, lacking confidence
Always second guessing
Always failing to adapt
Always seeking approval
Still not good enough
Weight of the world

On my shoulders, unbearable
Feeling awkward, don't belong
Stranger in the real world.

THE AWAKEN ONE

In a world gone astray
Only a few see the flaws
These blessed yet cursed souls
See and feel the world
For what it really is
This world is sick
But the masses are blind
Blind and ignorant
Cause ignorance is bliss.

The masses can't see and feel the world
The way the blessed yet cursed souls can
They are blessed cause they can see
What the ignorant masses can't see
They can feel what the ignorant masses can't feel
Yet they are cursed cause they are few
And the voice of the few
Don't matter in this world.

They are shunned and stigmatized
Alienated and pitied
Stereotyped as 'The Depressed'.

But they stand in the light
They see the world's darker side
They stand at the crossroads
And they see the true path
The world should have taken
The depressed are the awakened ones.

And if only the masses would see the world
Through the eyes of the awakened ones
If only the world is willing to listen
To the voice and cries of the awakened
Then there'd be a global awakening

The awakened ones would lead the world
Along the right and true path.

ADDICTION

I'm bound
I'm a captive
I'm a prisoner
Diabolical, fiendish, impious
Desires, holding me down
I want to break free
I want to be
Liberated, unshackled, released
Emancipate me from this bondage
I know it's possible
But how?
Who will?
What is there to be done?
Admonition, counsel, caution
Every time I'm falling into an abyss
Bottomless, endless chasm
I'm a convict
In this irony
Yet I can be free
But how?

BLESSING IN DISGUISE

In the blackness of life's darkness
In the bleakness of life's harshness
Lay treasures, concealed
That will only be revealed

When one has a will
As strong as a gale
That may blow away the blackness
Of life's darkness
And that one may brave the bleakness
Of life's harshness.

In the midst of life's infirmities
Induced by life's calamities
One that is willing to persevere
One that is willing to endure
Shall find the treasures of life concealed
In the midst of life's tribulations
Then let there be great jubilation
For one that is wise
Has found blessings in disguise.

MOMENTS IN MY LIFE

There are moments in my life
When the sun ceases to shine
Dark grey clouds fill my horizon
Thunder rumbles and lightning flashes
And rain falls with a mighty force
Then all hell breaks loose
And I'm carried away by the flood.

There are moments in my life
When I find myself
In the middle of no where
I'm left on my own device
It's like I'm trapped on an island
In the middle of the ocean
Where I find myself at world's end.

But there are also moments in my life
When the sun in my world
Shines so bright and with might
When it's light and warmth
I've craved so much
Gives me joy and strength.

Yes, there are also moments in my life
When I'm at peace with the whole world
As if all my problems just ceases to exist
And I'm encompassed with bliss and happiness.

PERPETUAL LIGHT

Where is the light?
Dim now is its radiance
Oh, how I crave its luminance
Where art thou, oh perpetual light?
Wilt thou shine in my darkest night?

Shine in the depths and dark places
Emancipate me from shackles of darkness
Liberate my soul from life's bleakness
Illuminate my path on a daily basis.

Oh gracious perpetual light
Please dim not your shine
Fade not, lest the dark of night
Seize the heart of mine.

TEARS OF JOY

Rain on my face
Droplets, heavenly torrent
Pelting, clearly God sent
Cleansing with such grace
Wiping the slate clean
Offering redemption
Forgiving all sins
No more damnation.

Rain on my face
Joy floods as tears
Removing my fears
There'll be better days
Of sunshine and happiness
No more guilt, no more pain
Second chances comes with the rain
When tears of joy fall down my face.

ACCEPTANCE

Battles can still be won
Without the need to fight
Fighting makes you weaker
It blinds you and limits your options.

Acceptance is the key
Allow what is to be
Reconcile, get used to it
Make your bed with tragedy
Make peace and make amends
And you shall know your enemy
Yield to pain and misery
Embrace it, do not fight it
Surrender, lay down your sword.

Calm the sea of your mind
Be still and you shall know
Your place, where you stand
Recognize your power
And you shall know yourself
You are the lord of your creation.

IN THE MIDDLE OF NOWHERE

There's a place within earth's realm
A place where all is pain and misery
A place of brokenness and emptiness
It's a place of nothingness
Just a place of empty space
Like in the middle of nowhere.

And if by infirmity, life sends you there
Rest assured, you're where you're supposed to be
Do not fear and do not lose hope
Just calm the sea of your mind
And weather the storms of life
Be still and you shall know
You are in the right place.

When the sands of chaos settle down
You'll find a place where all is still and calm
And peace, faith and assurance
Pervades the wide expanse
It's a place of peace and certainty
A place of strength and power
A place of self-discovery and identity
Where you shall know yourself
And you shall find yourself
In the middle of nowhere.

BRIEF ESCAPE

When the troubles of life become unbearable
I take a walk down to the white sandy beach
There I sit under my favorite red frangipani tree
The cool sea breeze blows against my face
It chills my spine and tastes of salt
I breathe in the sweet frangipani aroma
I watch the waves crash and the sea foam.

Right there for that moment only
I'm at peace with the whole world
As if all my problems just cease to exist
That is my brief escape from life's harsh realities.

HOPE

In the midst of my miseries
In this world of harsh realities
I often stumble in my struggles to cope
With problems that try to make me lose hope.

But I still hold on to the rope
And I always choose to cope
Because I know there is hope.

It is hope that keeps me enduring
It is hope that keeps me persevering
Hope is like an oasis in the desert
Hope is like a rope you hang on to.

You may have nothing
You may have no way to go
But if you have hope
It will never let you down.

Therefore, always nurture the hope
That there is hope
Cause there really is such a thing as hope.

POEMS IN MY HEART

There's a poem in my heart
For every pain in my life
My tears fall like drops of ink
On the pages of my heart
Where a poem is written
As a reminder to me
That pain is part of life.

There's also a poem in my heart
For every joy in my life
But it is not written with ink that fades
It is carved on the rock of my heart
Not as a reminder
But as a decree and promise
That there's a time
When pain will end.

WIND OF CHANGE

I heard the wind
Banging against my window
So I parted the curtains
And in pours the wind
As if it's delivering a message.

I don't know what the wind brought
But one thing I'm certain of is
The wind brought me relief.

Cause all day I sat in my room
With heavy thoughts running through my mind
That made me feel sick and depressed.

But that's all gone now
The wind has brought a change
To the way I think
To the way I feel
And to the way I view life.

Now I am not scared to walk
Out of my room and into the real world
Cause I know that the wind of change
Will always blow my way.

NO PAIN, NO GAIN

To every pain, there is a gain
Your efforts to fight will not be in vain
Challenged by limitations
Oppressed by tribulations
The whole world is against you
There's no way out; no escape
And yet you press on
No pain, no gain
That's the attitude.

You sail the raging seas
You climb the highest mountains
You head for the light
At the end of the tunnel
Surrounded by darkness and fear
You often stumble and fall
And yet you keep pressing on
No pain, no gain
That's the attitude.

And at last you reach the promise land
You are crowned with success and glory
You did it; nothing can stop you now
Against all odds you stood
You are invincible; you are incredible
You're a candle that burns in the rain.

A Prayer Away

On my bed I sat
With a burdened heart
And my eyes down cast
I felt emptiness
Descending on me
My heart ached.

So many troubles life brings
So many heart aches life's filled with.

On my bed I sat
And said a prayer to God
I asked him for his joy
To become the strength I needed so much.

Then the Lord spoke into my heart
He said to me son
You are not alone
I am always by your side
I'm just a prayer away.

THAT LITTLE VOICE

Sometimes in my solitude
When I'm lonely and I need
Someone to talk to and listen to
I often hear that little voice
Speaking to me in whispers
It's divine and soothing voice
Drives away all my fears.

I've tried to figure out where
That little voice comes from
I wonder whether it's carried by the wind
Or whether it's from deep inside my soul
Where this voice comes from is still a mystery.

But one thing I'm sure of is
That little voice seems familiar
It's as if I've known it all my life
And every time I hear that little voice speaking
I seem to hear my own voice.

It's like someone speaking to me
In my own voice
It's like me speaking to myself
Sometimes I wonder if it's my soul speaking to me
Or maybe God is speaking to me
Using my very own voice.

STORY OF MY LIFE

I live my life
One step at a time
With each pain and misery
I try to hope for the best
I'm always patient
I do what I have to do
To cope with each day's troubles
Tomorrow will worry about itself
Yesterday is gone, it's history
Today is all I have
So I make the most of it
As if it's the last day of my life.

Each day has its share of joy and pain
Each day is a new beginning
A new page of my life
I try to live only in the present moments
It's the only thing that matters.

One step at a time
I take a leap of faith
And hold on to my dreams
I hope they see the light of day
Nothing else matters.

I let the pain do its thing
Let it burn, let it hurt
Each time I heal
I become stronger than yesterday.

Life is a lesson, life is a gift
It's never too late
To start all over again today
Failure only exists in the grave
But I'm still alive

So I still I have a chance.

One day at a time
One step at a time
It's all I can do now
With each day as a new page
I write new chapters of my life.

I draw my inspiration
From my pain and misery
And I draw my strength
From the joy each day brings.

I live for one thing only
That is to make my dreams
See the light of day
To see them fulfilled and achieved
All chapters of my life completed
A book finally written
The story of my life.

EYE OF A TIGER

On the surface
I look sweaty and unsteady
But deep inside
I feel calm and ready.

I've weathered the storms
I've slayed the giants
I've overcome the impossible
And achieved the incredible
Now I'm truly invincible.

I am a fighter
I am a survivor
I am a warrior
I've got the eye of a tiger.

LIFE INVOLVES A CHOICE

My mind knows not
The reasoning of my heart
Its language and mysteries
Seem to baffle my mind.

My heart is calm and steady
It is patient and wholesome
Its reasoning, perfect and true.

But as for me, I stay where I am
Between my heart and my mind
Doing what I do best
Observing their interactions
Listening to their conversations
And doing what they tell me to do.

Most of the time
My mind controls me
It's very ambitious
I'm used to its loud voice.

But there are times
When I hear that little voice
Within me, speaking in whispers
So faint to hear
Sometimes I can't hear it
And this makes me restless
I'm lost and confused
I don't know whom to listen to
Should I listen to my mind?
Or should I listen to my heart?

I know my heart is always right
But sometimes it's hard to hear its voice
I know my mind always tell lies

But sometimes it tells the truth
Yet how can I tell
When it's telling the truth?

But life involves a choice
My life is based on choices I make
So I have to choose
What I think is right
What I think is true.

And only through the consequences
Of the choices I make
And the actions I take
Will I realize if I'm right or wrong.

TIME IS A PRISON

As I step onto the threshold
Where time fades into eternity
And get a glimpse of the timeless world
I realize that my deepest fear
And suspicion have always been true
I realize that I'm a prisoner after all.

I always feel like I'm trapped
I always feel like I'm stuck
And I'm kept as a prisoner.

In eternity, time ceases to exist
The past, the present and the future
Are all happening at the same time
And there's no order of events
I was surprised at what I saw.

But when I look back to my world
Which is governed and sustained by time
I see myself bound in the chains of time
I see myself stuck and trapped in the present
I can't go back to my past to change it
I can't even see into the future to know
What will happen to me.

Therefore, all I can say is
Time is a prison
And only eternity holds
The promise of freedom.

TANGIBLE HAPPINESS

I've been on a journey all my life
In pursuit of nothing but happiness
But it seems to me that I've been
Chasing after the wind
I've only had brief moments of happiness
That came my way but faded away
Just like the wind.

I could feel the happiness
But I just couldn't hold on to it
It always slipped through my hands
Just like the wind.

I've searched for a kind of happiness
That I could see with my eyes
One that I could feel
And grasp with my hands.

I've searched for a tangible happiness
So I may know that it's real
And I can own and keep with me
All the days of my life.

BETTER BLESSED LIFE

I close my eyes and pray
And hope for a better day
That I may find the way
To live a better life
In a world where badness is rife.

I pray and hope to receive
Wisdom and guidance to live
A life worthy of living
I know my heart is willing.

But it's my mind that lacks the will
Cause it's corrupt and it's ill
And it cannot clearly perceive
The right and proper way to achieve
A life free of transgression
And a life of happiness and satisfaction.

I pray with all my heart
That I may have the guts
To face all my fears and pain
So that I may finally gain.

Courage, strength and confidence
So that I can finally experience
The life I have hoped and prayed for
A life where pain and misery will be no more.

I pray with hope and with faith
Cause I know it's never too late
To have fate smile on me
So that happy and blessed I may be.

THERE'S MORE TO LIFE

There's more to life than we think we know
There's more to life than those tears
Streaming down your cheeks
There's more to life than your trials and tribulations
There's more to life than your pain and misery
Life ain't as bad as it seems
There's more to life than meets the eye.

There's so much more that life has to offer
More than enough to sustain our existence
More to thrill, excite and fascinate us
More to intrigue, inspire and surprise us
More to explore, discover and marvel at.

Life is full of mysteries
Life is full of possibilities
Life is full of happiness
Life is full of goodness
Life is full of hope
Life is full of love
Life is endless and unlimited
Life can never run out of supply
Life can never be depleted.

Therefore, we must embrace life
We must grasp it and never let go
We must believe and trust in life
We must expect more from life
We must never lose hope in life.

And if you think you know all about life
Think again, there's always a difference
Between what you know about life
And life as it really is
I mean there's just more to life.

IN SEARCH OF THE FLAME OF PASSION

Where is the passion I once had?
Where is the flame that once burned in my heart?
I have traveled the world over
In search of the flame; in search of passion
Like one who seeks a long lost love
I've stumbled upon treasures and riches
But these I do not seek
For what I seek is the flame
The eternal flame that burns
In the hearts of determined souls
And in the hearts of great men and women.

Oh precious sacred flame, my love
Where could you be, I wonder?
I have crossed oceans to find you
I have traveled around the world to find you
If only you could see me now
I'm frozen with this freezing deadness
My limbs are stiff and my heart is cold
And my mind has lost its wit
I am falling and dying
And only you can catch me
Only you can save me, my love.

Oh precious flame, my love
So sacred and treasured you are
Burn in my heart once again
Keep burning 'till I reach my destiny
You are the fuel of life itself
For you are the driving force within
Without you, I can achieve nothing.

So if I have to cross the oceans
If I have to travel the world over to find you
If I have to trade all my treasures just for you

Even if I have to sell my soul
I would do so just to have you
Burn in my heart once again.

You are the strength of my heart
You are the missing piece of my heart
I have the will but it's passion I need
Without the flame; without passion
I can will nothing; I can achieve nothing
Without passion, people perish.

MAKE ME A MIRROR

Chaos fills the depths of the soul
And time seems to stand still
There's no beginning and no end
Everything seems to be here and now
The past, the present and the future
Are all happening at the same time
And the soul is complete and free.

But the mind is restless
Still the mind is incomplete
And so it seeks some form of satisfaction
It seeks some form of explanations
The mind tries to create order
From the chaos within the soul
The mind tries to comprehend
The mysteries of the soul.

Now the soul also seeks to reveal its expressions
So the mind would understand its intentions
And gain completeness and satisfaction.

The mind, curious as it is, seeks
To know what it's like within the soul
It seeks to see the image of the soul
To see what it would look like
In this physical and tangible world.

Therefore, the mind interprets
The deep urges of the soul
And so the mind translates
The language of the soul
To feel what it's feeling
And to hear what it's saying

Now, if the mind listens carefully

It would hear the soul whispering:

"Make me a mirror
So I can see myself
And when you look in the mirror too
You would see my face; it's our face
Cause you'd be staring at yourself."

CONSCIOUSNESS

It is the state of being aware
The state of being awake
It is the knowing
To have knowledge of
To be a witness of
It is to have a will
To be free to choose.

Consciousness blinks
Like the seconds on the clock
It is a fragment of time
It is a spark of eternity
A glimpse into infinity
It is the heart beat
The pulse of the Universe.

I WISH I COULD FLY

I wish I could fly
Freely like the birds
High up in the sky
Oh what a release that would be
For my soul wants to be free.

I wish I could fly
Freely like the birds
With a cheerful heart
Oh what joy that would be
For my soul wants to be free.

I wish I could fly
Freely like the birds
No burdens, no heart aches
Only freedom to soar with the wind
And glide to my destiny.

PERCEPTIONS OF LIFE

Here I am standing
At the edge on the threshold
At the very precipice of life
Where its various realities intertwine
Where my perceptions of life as I know it
Seems to shatter and fade away
My very identity crumbles into a thousand pieces
And turns to dust in my hands
My identity is only a shadow of my perceptions
Standing here at the threshold
I realize that my life is just a perception
My life is an idea that needs to materialize
Like a dream that needs to see the light of day.

Here at the very precipices
My world my life
As I know it as I perceive it
Breaks away and fades into oblivion
My identity slips away and vanishes
I feel this emptiness descending on me
I feel this nothingness surrounding me
I feel like I'm dying
Yet I'm still alive
I feel like I'm a different person
I feel like I've been born again.

Standing here now at the edge
On the threshold at the very precipice
I see life in a very different way
I see life in a different light
Life is a thousand pieces of perception
Life is a chaotic mix of realities intertwined
So I pick up the new pieces
Pieces of my new life
And create a new perception of life

And with it a new identity
A new reality of life dawns on me.

And as I step back into the world
I can see a change
I can feel a change
But I just can't tell
If it's me who's changed
Or is it the world that has changed.

THE WORLD NEEDS LOVE

The world is home to people of
Many different languages and colored skins
And of people with different cultures
From which their belief springs
The world is made up of the blending
Of different civilizations
And the world is one global community
Consisting of many different nations.

But the world is divided by different ideologies and creed
Of religious sects, atheists, anarchists and many more
The world is full of people whose hearts
Are consumed by greed and the gap
Is getting wider between the rich and the poor.

The world has been plagued by wars, greed and inequality
 Still the world is divided by racism, hatred and lack of love
The world will achieve peace and unity
If only people change their mentality
And seek wisdom deep inside their hearts or from above.

The world is searching for solutions
To its problems and miseries
And for hope and answers to ease its pain and worries
The world needs to hear the message of love and hope
So that people inflicted with pain and misery can cope.

The world's problems will end if everyone's united
By one ideology or creed
One common philosophy or belief
That everyone will accept and heed
And only love is the perfect creed that will bring unity
So that the people of the world can live in peace and equality.

EQUALITY A POSSIBILITY

Anyone with perfect sanity
Can clearly see the possibility
That we can achieve equality
And live in peace and unity.

If only we respect each other's dignity
If only we live our lives in humility
And fill our hearts with love for humanity.

WHO AM I?

To get to the real essence of who I really am
I had to remove of a lot of labels
Labels I held on to because I wasn't too sure about myself
Labels that gave me a fake sense of belonging.

At first I took a long look at my name
My name is Bruce; Bruce is my name
Bruce, a one syllable word happens
To be a name that identifies me
It's a name people call me when they see me
Or talk about me
It's a name that comes to people's minds
When they think about me.

They say I'm Bruce; I say I'm Bruce
But am I? Am I just a mere word?
That people associate me with
When they see or think about me?
Or am I more than a word
Am I more than this one syllable
Verbal representation called Bruce.

And so it dawned on me
I'm not Bruce; I'm not a word
I'm more than a word
I'm flesh and blood and I'm real
I'm conscious; I think and feel
I breathe; I eat and have a will.

So who am I really?
When there's no word to label and identify me
How will I be identified; with only my face?
But then I'll be just a face in the crowd.
Who am I, really?
I mean deep inside of me at my very core

If I have a core; who am I really?
After every layer of my life has been peeled
What will remain of me?
What will be left of me that I can truly say is me?

And so I find myself on this epic quest
To discover who I really am
I mean after all, life is a journey; a voyage in the sea of life
Will I find myself at the end of this odyssey?
Or will there be nothing left of me
At the end of my life's journey?

So just who or what is 'Me' or 'I' that I'm looking for?
Maybe there isn't such a thing as 'Me'
Or 'I' that I can put a finger on
Even though I keep stripping away every label
Or layer in my life
I still haven't discovered who I really am yet.
I don't know if I'm ever close to
Or far from discovering my real identity; who I really am.

But if there's one thing that I'm beginning to be sure of
It's this:
In order to find out whom you really are
You must first find out who you really aren't.
And truth is, you really aren't all those things
You've labeled yourself with.

So now I stopped labeling myself
I'm peeling all these layers off
I'm no more Bruce or who I thought I was before
I still haven't found out who I really am yet
But for now I can only find little comfort
In realizing who I'm not
When I remove all these layers and labels off.

LIVE YOUR DREAMS

We measure our lives on earth
By the number of days we live
Days turn to weeks
Weeks turn to months
And months turn into years.

Ten years form a decade
And ten decades form a century
If you are lucky enough
You'll live more than a century.

It's the counting of years
That makes me feel different and older
My memories make me old
Each time I reflect back to the past
I feel a little bit different
A little bit mature, a little bit older.

But these are just days passing by
Like the clouds in the sky
My life shouldn't be measured
By days, months or years
It just doesn't make sense at all.

My life should be measured
By the dreams I achieve in this life
And by the goals I reach in this lifetime
By then I should at least know my purpose
Because life without purpose
Is life without meaning.

So it doesn't matter how long I should live
Leave the counting of years to the ignorant
All that matters is the dreams I have
And the will I have to achieve them

All men should live for their dreams
And by their dreams should their lives be measured.

LOVE IS THE ANSWER

I've tried to understand what exactly love is
And I'm beginning to understand it
Love is something that can be understood.

You can find it if you search for it
It is real and it is there
In fact, love is one of those things
That I am so sure of in life.

There are some things in life
That I'm not so sure about
And one of them is the existence of God
To search for God is like chasing the wind.

My conscious mind tells me
That I can never understand God
Or even the concept of his existence.

And what does my heart say?
Well, it says I'm not meant to
My heart tells me to pursue love instead
Cause that's what I'm meant to do.

I don't really know God
And what he's capable of
But I do know love
And what it is capable of
Cause I've seen what love has done.

Through the lives of those few individuals
Who have helped the poor, needy and homeless
Those who believe in the value of human life
Those who believe in peace and equality
That all men are created as equals.

We have expected God to end wars
We have prayed to God to end greed and poverty
We have prayed to God to end hatred and inequality
And we have turned a blind eye to love.

But if we would pursue love
And let our hearts be filled with it
If only we would yield to love
And let our hearts be consumed by its power.

Then we would come to realize
That we can solve the world's problems
That we can put an end to wars
That we can put an end to greed and poverty
And that we can put an end to hatred and inequality.

Cause love is the most powerful thing
In the whole world and universe
It can never be conquered by anything
But it can and will conquer all things
It is the ultimate solution to the world's problems.

Therefore, we must nurture that seed of love
That is planted in the soil of our hearts
Let its roots sink deep into our hearts
And let it bear fruits in our lives.

That's when love becomes complete
And perfected in our lives
When love is being perfected in us
We will then know what is truly right and wrong
We will then understand the meaning of life
And discover the ultimate reality of life itself.

Cause love can show the way
Only love can reveal the truth
Only through love can we live a perfect life

And I have found love
I realize that I have love inside my heart
It is inherent in me
It's been woven into my inner core
Like a seed, it has been planted
In the soil of my heart.

I have love at my disposal
I can feel it deep inside my heart
I know I am capable of loving
I'm absolutely sure of it.

Now if there's one thing that I'm sure of
It is that I'm not so sure about God
But I'm absolutely sure about love
And maybe by finding love, I have found God
Cause the Bible says God is love
And love is the answer for the world today.

I AM LIKE THE WIND

Whispers in the wind
Or voices from my heart
Deep within my soul
In my inner most being
Or perhaps just from my imaginations.

Is it a dream?
Or is it real
I cannot tell the difference.

I hear a sound; a voice perhaps
Words are spoken; yet so faint to hear
I try to listen to the voice
But it always fades away
Like a voice in a dream
Or the echoes in the wind.

But it was real!

I heard it; what were those words
Those whispered into my ears
Carried by the wind
From who knows where.

Oh it was real; I heard it
What were those words
That were spoken from deep within
My soul; in my inner-most being.

And as I begin to listen carefully
To the whispers in the wind
As I begin to listen earnestly
To the voice deep in my soul
In my inner-most being.

I can hear it calling my real name
It's telling me who I really am
That I am as free as the wind
I cannot be defined or labeled
That no one knows where I came from
And no one knows where I am going
Just like the wind blowing.

EARTH, OH EARTH

Earth, you're an island in the ocean of space
Earth, you're a pearl in the Milky Way
Earth, you're located at the perfect place
Earth, you're the place where people stay.

Earth, you're the cradle of human life
Earth, you're riddled with human strife
Earth, you're ravaged with war, greed and poverty
Earth, you're divided by hatred and inequality.

Earth, oh Mother Earth
I cry and pray for your salvation
Earth, you need love as your perfect solution.

POETRY

Poetry is my god
Poetry always delivers
Daily bread for the believer
That falls like shower
Oh sweet heavenly Manna
You give me power
And I will shout Hosanna!

Poetry is my religion
Thesaurus and dictionary, my Bible
I am the faithful disciple
Always eager to learn
I burn the mid night oil
And I labor and toil
To spread the poetry creed
To those willing to heed.

Poetry is my therapy
It's the best remedy
For my pain and misery
It's a medicine for loneliness
And redemption for my brokenness.

Poetry is a journey of self-discovery
It's a road less traveled
But I'll take the gamble
To seek personal attainment
So I may find enlightenment.

Poetry is my life
Like a faithful wife
And constant friend
The relationship never ends
Cause I've pledged my loyalty
When I fell in love with poetry.

FRIENDS FOREVER

Friendships that are struck with friends of different relations
Friendships that extend beyond the boundaries of blood
Even beyond the confines of distant family relations
Are forged to stand the test of time, it's a brotherhood.

He's like a brother, but from another mother
A mother having no relations to your father
Whether in love on in blood
But a mother who could've been your mother
And you both could've been brothers from the same father
It's like his mother who could've been your father's wife
But that probably would've been in another life.

These are friendships that are made in recognition
Of the each other's equivalence and like-mindedness
It's an acquaintance beyond the realm of comprehension
It's a brotherhood, a bold declaration of oneness
There's no division; no boundary and border to crossover
Only two people vowing to be united as friends forever.

ETERNAL SUNSHINE

As you set for the day
Precious being of light
You cast a last glance
And spread out your arms
In solemn rays
Offering comfort and courage
To the lonely travelers
And to the troubled sailors.

We bid you farewell
And thank you for the day's light
Take your rest and sleep well
Eternal sunshine.

EVENING SUN

Streaks of amber colored clouds
Paint the evening sky like a Monet
Crimson-red beams of sunlight reaches out
With outstretched arms, inviting me.

I feel the warmth of its dying flame
Gently caressing my face
The last solemn rays of the evening sun
Bathes me with its warmth
And beckons me with a whisper:

"Come away with me
Let's spend the night together."

I laugh and whisper back:

"Get some sleep
I'll see you in the morning."

SUN IN MY WORLD

As I gazed upon her beauty
I was amazed and blessed
Her beauty shines like the sun
For just as God said:

"Let there be light!"

There she was
Standing in front of me
She is the sun in my world
A sun that never sets.

When I first laid my eyes on her
I knew she was the one
And when she came into my life
She brought light into my world
She kindled the flame of my heart
Which shall burn eternally for her.

LOVE AT FIRST SIGHT

Food for thought
Feast for my eyes
A sight to behold
Object of obsession
Your beauty is.

Eye to eye
Heart to heart
Minds in sync
Mutual understanding.

It's bigger than us
Do not fight it
Let's go with the flow
And let love do its thing.

OUR DESTINY

Elegant, sweet delicate smile
Innocent, lovely pouting lips
Cherubic face with beautiful eyes
You bet your eyelids like butterfly wings
You launch your steps with amazing grace
But walk with a little attitude
I see you from a distance
And my heart skips a beat
Time stops ticking
I walk towards you.

Our eyes meet
I smile
You blush
We hug
We kiss.

I take your hand
You lean on me
And we walk towards our destiny.

LAY IN MY ARMS

Lay in my arms
It's where you belong
Cause when you're there
You are truly home
It's your home away from home.

Lay in my arms
There's no better place else
Where you could be
I'd shelter you and protect you
If that's what you'd want me to.

Lay in my arms
You know you want to
Don't resist, don't fight it
These arms were made to love you
So just say yes and let me hold you.

TRUTH IN YOUR EYES

Eyes never lie
They always tell the truth
Eyes are the windows to the soul
I see your soul in your eyes
And your eyes tell a story.

When I look into your eyes
I see the truth about us
I see that it's real
And that my mind and emotions
Aren't playing tricks on me.

The proof is in your eyes
Your soul speaks the truth
Our love is real
It would last a lifetime.

Cause when I look into your eyes
I see our future unfolding
I see the end; I see everything
Well, not exactly every little detail
But I see a happy ending for us.

LOVE OF A THOUSAND LIFETIMES

When I first saw her
I recognized her
Even though I've never met her
In this present life
But I knew that I knew her somehow
I knew I'd seen her before
But not in this world
Probably in another life
A life most definitely before this
I'm absolutely sure of it.

She was the one I was looking for
If I was searching for a woman
Then it would definitely be her
She reminded me of someone I knew
Someone not in this present lifetime
I'm absolutely sure of it.

Cause if I traveled the world over
I'd still not find someone exactly like her
So I must have seen and met her in my past life
In another place in an another time
This would be the only reasonable explanation.

And when I looked into her eyes
I saw her recognize me too
Somehow she knew me
Although I'm sure she knew
That she's never seen or met me before.

But she knew that
I knew she knew it too
It was obvious to us
Yet we both couldn't explain it
It was bigger than us

And we just couldn't deny it
Nor could we fight it.

It was fate, it was destiny
We were both sure of it
No one could convince us otherwise
I had found her and she had found me
We both had found something that people
Would search for all their lives
And in different lifetimes.

We had found something that
All people born on earth
Are meant to find some time in their lifetime
Life without it would have no meaning
Life would have no fun and purpose
And there'd be no reason to live at all.

But we both have a reason to live for
I'd live for her and she'd live for me
That, we both knew in our hearts
It's the only thing that matters
Nothing else matters any more
We both had found love.

I knew it when I first saw her
I knew I had found not just the love of a lifetime
But the love of a thousand lifetimes
And I knew she knew it too.

A LIFETIME OF LOVE

Love is in the air
Love is all around
Enchanted by its charms
We're both under its spell.

Under the moonlight's watch
I lay you down on a bed
Of a thousand rose petals
And become one with you
Our passions ignite
Our souls entwine
And we coil like two serpents
In our garden of eden
The center of our universe
And the birthplace of our souls.

In this ocean of love
We make magic
We make love
So fiercely, sending ripples and waves.

Yes we make love
On a bed of a thousand stars
So fiercely, so passionately
We burn the stars with our love's flames
They fall as shooting stars
To inspire the hopeless romantics.

Tonight is just you and me
Nothing else matters anymore
This moment right here
Is a lifetime of love
Cause in loving you
Would be the end of life as I know it.

A WOMAN TO LOVE

Blissful heavenly kiss
Proceeds from your lips
Words of love you whisper
So softly and tenderly
Into my ear
'Till I faint with love.

Come my love
Let me embrace you
Come my love
Let me touch you
And let me love you
For you are a woman to love.

WHEN SHE SMILES

She amazes me with her smile
Her delicate lips curve beautifully
Like an inverted rainbow
She smiles and the sun shines
She's a rare sunshine on a cloudy day
And the warmth of her smile
Drives away the cold.

She smiles cause she knows
The effect her smile has on me
She steals my attention like it's a treasure
With her hypnotic smile
She tortures me with those killing smiles
Each time she did, the world ended
I mean, my world ended.

But then she would smile again
And there'd be a new beginning
She brings light with her blushing smile
Her lips curve like a crescent moon
And shines in my darkest nights.

When she smiles I smile
I can't help it, it's contagious
And there's no cure to it
But it doesn't kill me
If anything, it heals me
And makes me whole again.

BROKEN BY YOU

My heart, it is broken
Crushed by my love for you
I simply can't help it
I wonder if I really have a choice here
I'm helpless, I'm at your mercy.

Only you can mend
The broken pieces of my heart
And you would know how to
I mean, you should know how to
Cause it was broken by you.

On a Desolate Beach

On a desolate beach
We both lay on the sand
Cuddled in blissful ignorance
We were at peace with life
Basking in the present moment
Time stood still; the world paused
Only this moment was real.

We could hear the waves crash
We could see the seagulls fly
The sea breeze tasted of salt
The air was scented with frangipani
This moment here was real
It was a dream that came true.

And as she laid in my arms
I sniffed the scent of her skin
I breathed her in and came alive
She is pure oxygen
She gives life with her mouth
Her lips are soft, her kisses are sweet
And her dancing eyes, full of promises.

I glanced away from her
And I asked myself two questions:
Do I really deserve her?
Am I good enough for her?
Then I glanced back at her
She was looking at me all this time
Our eyes met and never parted
And that was the moment
When I saw it in her eyes
She had already asked herself
The very same two questions.

So we lay on the sand
Cuddled in blissful ignorance
We had found the moment of truth
We had found each other
On a desolate beach.

The Fall of Niugini

Oh Niugini, land of mysticism and superstition
Land of a thousand gods and black magic
Land of warriors and legends
Land of mountain ranges and vibrant volcanoes
Land of mangroves, swamps and rainforests
Land of mighty rivers and white sandy beaches
Land of a thousand tribes and tongues
And home of the Birds of Paradise
Which rule over our skies with pride.

Oh Niugini, you were once a Garden of Eden
An ancient paradise for our ancestors
You are the mother land, the cradle of life
You are our origin, our genesis
Where our civilization had its beginning.

Oh Niugini, you were so beautiful and virgin
You were a sight to behold and adore
But your beauty is now your curse
Cause the serpent has craved for you with lust
And has deceived and poisoned the minds
And hearts of your very own people
Whom you cared for as your off springs
With promises of a greater and better life
A life so tempting yet with a darker side to it.

Oh Niugini, now you're not so beautiful or virgin anymore
You're not a sight to behold and adore anymore
The serpent has defiled you and stripped off your beauty
Your mountain ranges have been mined for its gold
Your rivers and seas are polluted by toxic chemical wastes
Your rainforests are being cut and destroyed every day.

Oh Niugini, you've been sold out by your people
You've been forced to be the serpent's bride

Every time I see you, I turn my face away
It's not that I'm ashamed of you
It's because I'm ashamed of what we have done to you.

Oh Niugini, I cry and pray that we your people
May see your pain and hear your cries
That we will have a change of heart and take you back
And chase the serpent away from you
To save whatever dignity that is left of you.

Motherland

This land., this once mysterious Island
That kings conspired to claim as their possession
That merchants sought to steal its treasures
That kings claimed as their footstool
And kingdoms waged war and fought for.

So much blood have been spilled on this land
But it was the blood of the foreigners
Fathers and sons who left their wives and mothers
To fight for kingdom, crown and glory.

This land, this mysterious island of dark secrets
Of stories and legends only told by word of mouth
In the *haus-mans* and *haus-tambarans*
Only at nights and around the fire.

This land is the birth place, the land of genesis
The place of origin for our first ancestors
Who lived along its white sandy beaches
Who dwelt in its highlands and mountains.

This land is like an inheritance passed on
From generations to generations
It's a possession that truly can't be owned
Instead it owns us, it lays claim to our identity
Like how a mother claims that a child is hers.

This land where we were born, will live on and die
This land where we make our gardens, hunt and fish
And where we build our houses and raise our children
This land is like a mother, we'll call it our Motherland.

THOUSAND CARAT DIAMOND

Can you hear the sound?
Carried by the trade winds
Can you hear the sound?
Of the *kundu* and *garamut*
Of the conch shell and bamboo flutes.

It is the sound of invitation
It is a calling for an audience.

Can you see the sign in the sky?
It is the Southern cross
The signal of invitation
Can you see the sign in the sky?
It is the bird of paradise
Calling for an audience.

Follow the sound of the *kundu*
(*kam-kam…kam-kam…kam-kam*)
'Come...come...come and see!'
'Come...come...you have to see!'

Follow the sound of the *garamut*
Follow the stars in the sky
Follow the bird of paradise
'Come...come...come and see!'
'Come...come...oh you must see!'
Come to the south pacific
Come to the island of new guinea
Come to the land of paradise
Come to papua new guinea
Come and see for yourself
This is the only day you will see
The display of a thousand carat diamond
Melanesian princess
The tropical sun paints your skin dark

The tapa cloth and grass skirt covers your nakedness
The frangipani and hibiscus flowers grace your ears
The tropical coconut oil polishes your skin.

You walk along the white sandy beaches
With your hair flailing in the cool sea breeze
Like palm trees in the wind, you sway your hips
From side to side as you dance to the beat
Of the *kundu* drums and *garamut*.

You are a butterfly of niugini
You're the black rose of melanesia
You are the pearl of south pacific
You are a treasure to be discovered.

So protect your beauty and your dignity
Cherish your family and help your community
Respect your roots and accept your identity
As a true melanesian princess.

THE SIMPLE LIFE

All I want
Is a simple life
A cabin by the lake
Out in the country side
With land to make garden
Bush to hunt wild games
And the best fishing spots.

I'm just a simple guy
I just want simple things
A small library in my cabin
Filled with all my favorite books
A piano and an acoustic guitar
To make sweet soulful music
And a small sound system
To hear my favorite songs
Is it too much to ask for?

I'm not asking for fame
Or a lot of money
Cause I have realized
That the very best things in life
Don't cost a thing
They are freely given.

The smile on your wife's face
The sound of your kid's laughter
The cries of a new born baby
The joy of playing with your pet
Watching the sun rise and sun set.

There'd still be an endless list
Of priceless things and moments
That'll take your breath away
But won't cost you a thing

And you can have them all
Only if you choose the simple life.

LONELINESS

Loneliness is like an island
In the midst of the ocean
They say that no man is an island
But when a man is lonely
He really is an island.

LYING EYES

Eyes
Yeah, those eyes
Those lovely lying eyes
They always give you away
You say no
But I can see it
In your eyes
And it's
Yes.

ABOUT THE AUTHOR

Born on May 6, 1985, Bruce is the third and last born son of Sarah and Jacob Kokoreso. He comes from Kainantu in the Eastern Highlands Province and Bensbach, Morehead in the Western Province of Papua New Guinea. His childhood was spent in some of the most remote outstations in Western Province where his father had served as a community and primary school headmaster.

Bruce completed his secondary education at Kiunga Secondary school and was awarded a scholarship to study Management and Accounting at the Pacific Adventist University.

www.ingramcontent.com/pod-product-compliance
Lightning Source LLC
LaVergne TN
LVHW051705080426
835511LV00017B/2742